The Lord God made
And did not rest
When He considered
MY life
He considered what's best!!

"For I know the plans I have for you," declares the LORD, "plans to prosper you and not to harm you, plans to give you hope and a future." Jeremiah 29:11

He knows the plans
All that He has for me
Plans for good
and not evil
Plans for prosperity!

Job 23:12
I have not departed from the command of His lips; I have treasured the words of His mouth more than my daily bread.

He loves me and
Gives me a plan in
His Word
He wants me to see
Clearly and to live
What I've heard!

There is one however...
Who wants to kill and to steal
My life and my heart
So I'll stay in his will

He confuses and twists
Everything in our head
So be careful to listen
To the Bible instead

For if we rely
On our own feelings
or thoughts
We will find ourselves
Questioning everything
That we're taught

Next thing that you know
That plan will soon die
And a new plan will live
In your heart as a lie

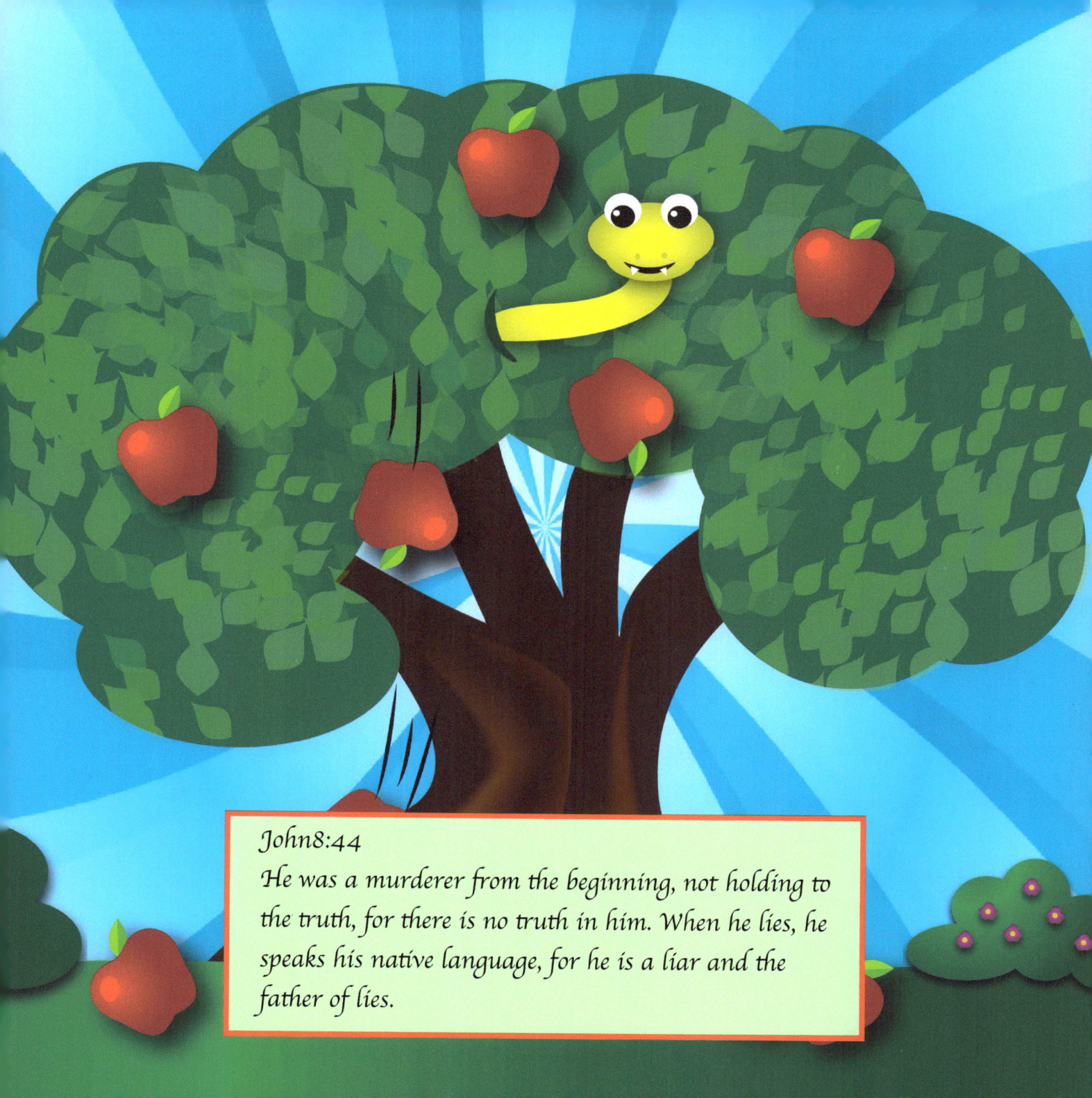

Your life may seem good
And you may feel like
you're free
You may think
you are being
What you were
Created to be

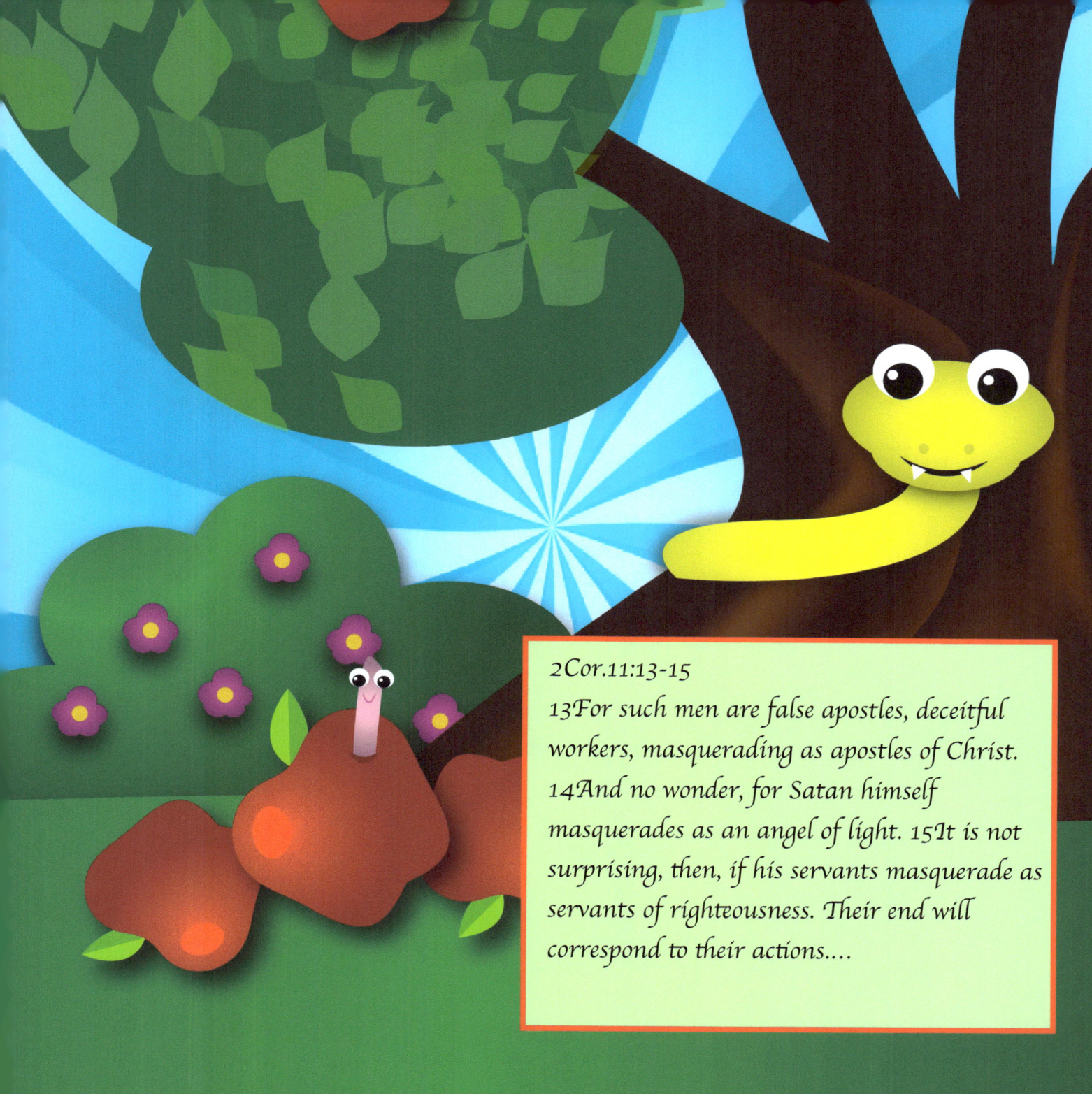

But you will have missed
What God had for you
If you had followed and trusted
His Word to be true

John1:1

1In the beginning was the Word, and the Word was with God, and the Word was God. 2He was with God in the beginning. 3Through Him all things were made, and without Him nothing was made that has been made..... Believing in Jesus is living the WORD!

So remember this life
here on earth
Is only a test
A moment in time
Before these bodies
Will rest

Philippians 3:20
But our citizenship is in heaven, and from it we await a Savior, the Lord Jesus Christ,

So stay true to the one
Who is true to the end
Our Lord God Almighty
Faithful Father
And Friend

James 1:17 17
Every good and perfect gift is from above, coming down from the Father of the heavenly lights, who does not change like shifting shadows.

Written by Amy Norris
Illustrated by
Alexis Olguin & Amy Norris

©2017trainupachildminsitries.com
Reservation of Rights
ISBN - 978-0-692-92640-6

www.trainupachildministries.com